What Is the Great Commission?

Crucial Questions booklets provide a quick introduction to definitive Christian truths. This expanding collection includes titles such as:

Who Is Jesus?

Can I Trust the Bible?

Does Prayer Change Things?

Can I Know God's Will?

How Should I Live in This World?

What Does It Mean to Be Born Again?

Can I Be Sure I'm Saved?

What Is Faith?

What Can I Do with My Guilt?

What Is the Trinity?

TO BROWSE THE REST OF THE SERIES, PLEASE VISIT: **LIGONIER.ORG/CQ**

CQ

What Is the Great Commission?

R.C. SPROUL

 LIGONIER MINISTRIES

What Is the Great Commission?
© 2015 by R.C. Sproul

Published by Ligonier Ministries
421 Ligonier Court, Sanford, FL 32771
Ligonier.org

Printed in China
RR Donnelley
0001121
First edition, eighth printing

ISBN 978-1-64289-056-3 (Paperback)
ISBN 978-1-64289-084-6 (ePub)
ISBN 978-1-64289-112-6 (Kindle)

Cover design: Ligonier Creative
Interior typeset: Katherine Lloyd, The DESK

Scripture quotations are from the ESV® Bible (The Holy Bible, English
Standard Version®), copyright © 2001 by Crossway, a publishing ministry of
Good News Publishers. Used by permission. All rights reserved.

The Library of Congress has cataloged the Reformation Trust edition as follows:
Sproul, R.C. (Robert Charles), 1939-2017
 What is the great commission? / by R.C. Sproul.
    pages cm. -- (Crucial questions series ; No. 21)
 ISBN 978-1-56769-498-7
1. Great Commission (Bible) I. Title.
 BV2074.S67 2015
 269'.2--dc23

                              2015018382

Contents

Chapter One

What Is
the Gospel?

The battle between the Persian army of Darius I and the troops of Greece that took place at Marathon in 490 BC was a watershed moment in the Greco-Persian Wars and in the history of Western society. Until that point, Darius had not been defeated in his quest to conquer Greece, and Persian dominance across the Mediterranean region had grown steadily for more than one hundred and fifty years. The defeat of the superior Persian forces by the Greek army at Marathon ushered in the two-hundred-year influence of Classical Greek culture and the decline of the Medo-Persian Empire.

This was a hugely important battle—yet the people back home had no idea of the outcome in the battle's immediate aftermath. They had to wait anxiously to get some word of what had happened. But today, in most cases, we don't have to wait very long for updates on significant events. We live in a world where news travels very rapidly, with sophisticated technology to announce what is going on around the globe in a matter of moments. In the ancient world, though, it was not like that. A battle of strategic importance for the history of the nation may have been taking place two thousand miles away, and it would certainly have taken some time for reports to travel so far.

Armies in the ancient world used runners to carry word about the outcome of battles. The people at home would post lookouts to watch for some sign of a messenger. It's said that the watchman could tell by the bearing of the runner whether he was coming with good news or bad.

One of the enduring legacies of the Battle of Marathon is as the inspiration of the marathon-length race. The legend is that a runner brought news of the Athenian victory to the city of Athens and dropped dead from exhaustion after he arrived. He pushed himself to the absolute limit because he was bearing good news, and he wanted the people to be able to rejoice in it.

The Apostle Paul alluded to these practices in his epistle to the Romans, where he said, "How beautiful are the feet of those who preach the good news!" (10:15). Picture how the watchman could see the feet flying as the runner rushed to the city gates to bring good news. It was a beautiful sight, and the people would shout celebrations of victory at the sight of him. They had a word for that kind of a message: it was a *euangelion*, a good message—a *gospel*.

The word *gospel* derives from the Old English *godspell*, meaning "good story" or "good message." *Godspell* translates the Latin *evangelium*, which is derived from the Greek *euangelion*. The Greek word is made up of the prefix *eu-* and the root *angelion*. The prefix *eu-* is found frequently in the English language and refers to something "good." Take the word *euphemism*, for example. A dentist about to drill might say, "This may cause a bit of discomfort," rather than, "This is going to hurt." He uses softer words to take the edge off something that is difficult for us to hear. That's a euphemism: stating something in better terms than it actually is. Likewise, at a funeral, when a minister stands up and says something nice about the deceased, we call that a *eulogy*, a "good word."

When that prefix *eu-* is added to the root *angelion*, which means "message" (the same root gives us the word "angel" or "messenger"), we get *euangelion*, "good message." Originally, the word *euangelion* functioned as a literal expression for any good report—particularly in the context of military engagements or political campaigns. But when we come to the New Testament, the concept of a *euangelion* takes on a new meaning. Jesus began His ministry with a public proclamation about good news that He was announcing to the people: what we call the gospel of the kingdom. He declared a new state of affairs, which He illustrated in many different ways with parables, saying "the kingdom of heaven is like this" or "the kingdom of God is like that."

By the time that we get to the Epistles, we see that the usage of *euangelion* or *gospel* undergoes a change. After the personal ministry of Jesus—after His life, death, and resurrection—the New Testament writers no longer speak about the gospel of the kingdom. Instead, they talk about "the gospel of Jesus Christ." Apostolic preaching was focused on the person and the work of Jesus. That's what the word *euangelion* came to mean by the close of the New

Testament: it had to do with a message and announcement about Jesus, including who He was and what He did.

We read of this gospel in Luke 24:

> But on the first day of the week, at early dawn, they went to the tomb, taking the spices they had prepared. And they found the stone rolled away from the tomb, but when they went in they did not find the body of the Lord Jesus. While they were perplexed about this, behold, two men stood by them in dazzling apparel. And as they were frightened and bowed their faces to the ground, the men said to them, "Why do you seek the living among the dead? He is not here, but has risen. Remember how he told you, while he was still in Galilee, that the Son of Man must be delivered into the hands of sinful men and be crucified and on the third day rise." And they remembered his words, and returning from the tomb they told all these things to the eleven and to all the rest. (Luke 24:1–9)

Think about what it was like for the Eleven when these women came running back from the tomb and in their excitement said to them, "He's not there, but He has arisen." This message was not just *any* good news. It was not just a word of a victory in battle or the announcement of a political hero's election. This was the greatest message that had ever been communicated to the world. This was an announcement that changed everything. If this message is true, it *has* to change everything. You cannot hear it and be indifferent. That's why people are often so hostile to the proclamation of the gospel: they understand that if it is true, life can never be the same.

The key to understanding the importance of the gospel is found in the first verse of the book of Romans, when Paul identifies himself as "Paul, an apostle, a slave of Jesus Christ set apart for the gospel of God" (1:1). When Paul speaks about the gospel of God, he is not saying that it is a message *about* God, but that it is a message that *belongs* to God. In other words, he's saying that this gospel comes to us *from* God. It is God who declared Christ to be the Messiah by raising Him from the dead. It is God who announces to the world the essence of what we call the *kerygma*: the proclamation of the life, death, resurrection, ascension, and return of Christ. So, then, the whole task of evangelism is merely to repeat to the world what God Himself has first declared. He was the original messenger.

What is the nature of this message? During the nineteenth century, there was a period of skepticism about the reliability of Scripture and about many of Scripture's claims regarding supernatural events such as miracles. In response, some reduced the meaning of Christianity to the ethical core of the teaching of Jesus, claiming that what matters is not Jesus' supernatural status or authority, but rather the power and relevance of His teachings. According to this interpretation, the real gospel has to do with the message of Jesus for human relationships, because He taught people how to get along with one another. This perspective came to be known as the "social gospel"; it beckoned the church to a new mission of getting involved with social justice and caring for the sick, the poor, the dying, and the oppressed.

But if we are basing our definition of *gospel* on the New Testament sense of the word, then there is no room for a merely social gospel. The gospel in the New Testament, first and foremost, is a message about a person and about what He accomplished through His life, death, resurrection, and ascension. This does not mean that the church should not be concerned with ethics and social justice, for if the gospel of Christ is true, the social implications are staggering. In fact, it is because of that gospel that the church must become conscious of the needs of those who are broken and hurting. But we can never replace the message of Christ with a human enterprise of social concern. Our social concern *flows out of* the gospel—it does not *replace* the gospel.

The gospel, in its essence, is an announcement about Jesus, who Himself embodies the breakthrough into history of the kingdom of God. The good news of the New Testament starts as a message about the kingdom and ends as the message of the King.

Chapter Two

What Is
Evangelism?

Martin Luther once said, "Every Christian must become Christ to his neighbor." Was he suggesting that each Christian should die on a cross to atone for the sins of his neighbors? No, he was saying that Christ is invisible to our unbelieving neighbors. They don't see the cross, the empty tomb, or the transfigured Jesus. They don't see Him in His ascended glory, and they don't see Him at the right hand of the Father. All they see is you and me—and in seeing us, they must see Christ.

That picture of how we relate to Christ—and how Christ relates through us to others—has always meant something to me. When I was converted, it was through a man who told me about Christ, and though I can't remember a word he said, I saw the power of Christ in him. When I saw it, I knew that I had to have it, whatever it was (I certainly didn't know at the time). He was a faithful witness to Christ.

What does it mean to be a witness to Christ? What is evangelism? Are they the same thing? The word *evangelism* obviously has something to do with the *evangel*, the good message. Evangelism, in its simplest definition, is "gospeling" or "making the gospel known."

The Great Commission in Matthew's gospel is one of the church's great charters for evangelism. It reads:

Now the eleven disciples went to Galilee, to the mountain to which Jesus had directed them. And when they saw him they worshiped him, but some doubted. And Jesus came and said to them, "All authority in heaven and on earth has been given to me. Go therefore and make disciples of all nations, baptizing them in the name of the Father and of the Son and of the Holy Spirit, teaching them to observe all that I have commanded you. And behold, I am with you always, to the end of the age." (Matt. 28:16–20)

Notice that Jesus prefaces this commission by announcing to His disciples that He has been given all authority on heaven and earth. The impetus for the task of the church to be involved in evangelism resides in the authority of Christ, who commands that the church be engaged in certain kinds of activity.

In recent years, discussion has emerged on whether evangelism is even an appropriate enterprise of the church. Yet it seems unthinkable to me that a church should consider whether evangelism is an appropriate enterprise when it has the mandate of the authoritative command of the Lord and Head of the church.

Why has this become a debatable point? Emil Brunner gave one answer in *The Mediator*, his classic work on Christ. Brunner lashed out at the modern church, saying that the issues of nineteenth-century liberalism, for example, are not a matter of technical debates about minor points of doctrine. Rather, the question is essentially one of unbelief, and we have to recognize that we do live in a time when there is a great deal of unbelief, not only outside the church but inside it as well. When strong unbelief is present, the church's vision, zeal, passion, and commitment for evangelism tend to decline. Who would be zealous about urging other people to believe something that they themselves do not believe?

But it would be simplistic to assume that every discussion about the legitimacy of evangelism resides in unbelief. That's certainly a factor, but there are other reasons as well. In many circles, evangelism has a bad name because it conjures up ideas of high-pressure techniques, simplistic buttonholing, and insensitive forms of communication. For others, evangelism implies those high-powered sales pitches that almost intimidate or manipulate people into "responding" in the way the salesperson desires. But that's not what the Bible teaches us about evangelism.

The Bible teaches that evangelism is the proclamation of the gospel to the whole world. That task is still central to the mission of the church. But notice in Matthew's account that Jesus is not just interested in declaring a simple message. He goes beyond that, saying, "Make disciples." The Greek word translated "disciple," *mathētēs*, means "one who is a learner or student." It's part of the church's mission to be involved in instructing and catechizing—that is, in discipling—people; this involves not just asking for an initial commitment, but rooting and grounding people in the whole counsel of God. But there's some overlap between discipling, evangelism, teaching, and so on, which we can see as we consider the mandate given to the church in the opening chapter of the book of Acts.

As Jesus prepared to ascend into heaven, He gathered His disciples around Him. During this last opportunity to speak with Him as a person on earth, the disciples asked Him a question: "Lord, will you at this time restore the kingdom to Israel?" (Acts 1:6). In other words, was He going to be the messiah they had been hoping from the beginning that He would be? Jesus does not disparage them by saying, "How many times do I have to tell you I'm not going to restore the kingdom to Israel?" What He says is very important for understanding the mission of the church:

It is not for you to know times or seasons that the Father has fixed by his own authority. But you will receive power when the Holy Spirit has come upon you, and you will be my witnesses in Jerusalem and in all Judea and Samaria, and to the end of the earth. (Acts 1:8)

Jesus tells the disciples, first of all, that there are certain things that are in the hands of the Father that are none of their business; nothing can frustrate His plans, so they should quit worrying about it. But then, He gives them a mandate: "You will be my witnesses." Often, people use the verb *to witness* interchangeably with the verb *to evangelize*, as if the two words were synonyms. But these terms do not mean the same thing in the New Testament, though they are certainly intimately and inseparably related. In the New Testament, witnessing is a generic word that encompasses different kinds of ways of communicating the gospel—and one of these ways is evangelism.

Therefore, all evangelism is witness, but not all witness is evangelism. Evangelism is a special kind of witness. To bear witness to something, according to the New Testament, is to call attention to it. The word for "witness" in Greek is *martyria*, from which we get the English word "martyr." New Testament Christians understood that one way that they called attention to the truth of Christ, one way they sought to make visible the invisible kingdom, that is, to bear witness to it, was by dying for it. They made manifest something that was invisible to their unbelieving neighbors.

Jesus was leaving, going to the right hand of the Father, to His coronation. He was going to be crowned the King of that kingdom that He had announced. But we don't see the kingdom; it's invisible. You can't look up in the sky and see Jesus sitting on a throne. Some people have sought to spiritualize the kingdom altogether, saying, "It's something that's in the hearts of men." No, the kingdom of God is an objective reality, not just a subjective feeling—but it's invisible. So, what is the church's task? To make visible the invisible kingdom of God. That's what witnessing is all about.

To witness means that you show people something they don't see. There are many ways to do this, according to Scripture. When we celebrate the Lord's Supper, we're doing something visible that shows forth the Lord's death until He comes. Jesus spoke of another way to witness: "By this all people will know that you are my disciples, if you have love for one another" (John 13:35). The way Christians relate to each other—which is something that people can see—bears witness to Christ. When we feed the hungry, clothe the naked, and visit the imprisoned, we bear witness to the compassion of Christ. The Christian, without converting people to Christ, can still bear witness to who Jesus is and what He is like.

There's a certain sense in which the bearing of witness to the kingdom of Christ is every human being's God-given responsibility, because every human being is made in the image of God. To be made in the image of God is to demonstrate to the whole creation the character of God. But since the fall, the image of God in man has been obscured; we have not reflected and mirrored the holiness of God to a fallen world.

Evangelism, on the other hand, is the actual proclamation—either oral or written, but certainly verbal—of the gospel. It is declaring the message of the person and work of Christ, who He is and what He has done on behalf of sinners like you and me.

That means there are several things that evangelism is *not*. It is not living your life as an example. It is not building relationships with people. It is not giving one's personal testimony. And it is not inviting someone to church. These things may be good and helpful, but they are not evangelism. They may lay the groundwork for evangelism. They may allow others to relate to us, or they may cause someone to be curious about why we live the way we do. But they are not evangelism, because they don't proclaim the gospel. They may say something about Jesus, but they do not proclaim the person and work of Christ.

When we consider our own role in witnessing and evangelism, we have to be careful that we're not only doing pre-evangelism and making appointments for other people to do evangelism, and that we aren't simply being a silent witness. We must be sure that the church is fulfilling its mandate to do evangelism, which is the actual proclamation of the person and work of Christ. *That's* the message that God has endowed with power, through which He has chosen the foolishness of preaching to save the world. It's the "power of God for salvation," as the Apostle Paul described it (Rom. 1:16).

Not every Christian is called to be an evangelist. In the New Testament, we see the church defined as a body with unity in diversity; the Holy Spirit gives gifts to every member of the body of Christ. Every single person in the church has been gifted by the Holy Spirit to do and perform some task to bear witness to Christ. There are teachers, evangelists, administrators, and a host of other offices that Christ establishes in His church. Everyone, no matter their gift, must be willing to make a confession of faith themselves. But not everyone is called to be what the New Testament calls an evangelist, someone who focuses on proclaiming the gospel of Christ.

Some may give a sigh of relief, noting the difficulty they have with telling others about their faith. But remember this: every Christian must be willing to confess Christ with their mouths, or they're far from the kingdom. Likewise, it is every Christian's duty to make sure that the task of evangelism is done. Are all teachers? No—but it is your responsibility as a member of the body of Christ to make sure that teaching is done. Is everyone a missionary? No—but it is your responsibility to make sure that the missionary enterprise is carried out. So, we all have a part in the responsibility of the whole mission of the church.

There is no enterprise that's more exciting than evangelism. I'm not an evangelist; I'm a teacher. It seems obvious to me and to those who know me that my gift and calling is to teach. When I was a new Christian, I first volunteered to be an evangelist; God said "no." Next, I wanted to be a missionary; God said "no" again. I did not want to be a teacher; but I probably talked to a thousand people one-on-one about Jesus Christ before I ever saw a single person respond to the gospel. There's still a sense in which I have the heart of an evangelist, and I care about evangelists, but it is not my gift.

We know that only the Holy Spirit can change a heart; but to be used by God to communicate that gospel to a human being—is there any greater privilege in this world than that? If the man who led me to Christ were convicted of murder in the first degree, or if he scandalized the Christian community by unbecoming conduct, or repudiated his friendship with me, I would still be eternally grateful that he opened his mouth and taught me about Christ. When I think of him, I think again of that text, "How beautiful are the feet of those who preach the good news!"

Chapter Three

Mobilizing
the Laity

O n a trip to Israel to visit the geographic sites of the Old
and New Testaments, I was fascinated to see the situation in Israel. This country, of course, has been a place of strife for decades. We saw people in civilian clothes walking down the street with guns over their shoulders. There were men on the beaches in bathing suits with submachine guns strapped across their bodies. Traveling through the Golan Heights, we saw signs along the roads warning that the fields were full of land mines. We saw plenty of other military

activity as well. It seemed so incongruous: daily life was going on in a routine fashion, yet there was always a threat of military confrontation that could come at any moment.

What was most interesting about the military situation in Israel was how this small nation has to be prepared for the possibility of a military encounter at virtually any moment, and how it is fully committed to a state of military preparedness. Upon graduation from high school, every male in Israel is required to enter the military for three years of service. Every graduating female is required to go into the service for two years. After the time of service is up, they're still required to spend one month out of every year in reserve training until age fifty-one. There's a sense in which every citizen is always considered a part of the army.

In Israel, military preparedness is the norm. And the New Testament indicates that something similar is expected of the church. While it is not the militancy of the sword, the imagery in the Scriptures and on the lips of Jesus in describing the mission of the church is borrowed from the military world. An army's readiness is one of its most important qualities, and it seems that the church today certainly has an adequate number of troops. We have considerable training opportunities available to us.

What we lack is the ability to come together for action—to be mobilized.

Often, it is assumed that the best way to carry out the mission of the church is to hire a preacher or a ministerial staff and let them handle the engagements necessary for the battle to be won. But have you ever heard of an army whose general was the only one in the fight? For an army to be successful, it has to have a skilled, trained, and mobilized rank-and-file. That's no less true in the kingdom of God, and in the warfare that is not against flesh and blood but against rulers and authorities and spiritual forces of evil (Eph. 6:12).

There are some important biblical texts that speak to the issue of the mobilization of the laity. One of the most important ones is found in Exodus, in the account of Moses' being visited by his father-in-law, Jethro. It begins:

> The next day Moses sat to judge the people, and the people stood around Moses from morning till evening. When Moses' father-in-law saw all that he was doing for the people, he said, "What is this that you are doing for the people? Why do you sit alone, and all the people stand around you from morning till evening?" And Moses said to his father-in-law,

"Because the people come to me to inquire of God; when they have a dispute, they come to me and I decide between one person and another, and I make them know the statutes of God and his laws." (Ex. 18:13–16)

Jethro saw Moses ministering to the people all day long. He scratched his head and said, "Moses, what are you doing?" We can almost read between the lines here and detect the slightest hint of pride on Moses' part, or at least a sense of a feeling of accomplishment of a job well done, as he explains his crucial role in leading and judging the people.

Instead of congratulating Moses, Jethro lectured him:

Moses' father-in-law said to him, "What you are doing is not good. You and the people with you will certainly wear yourselves out, for the thing is too heavy for you. You are not able to do it alone." (vv. 17–18)

Notice that Jethro didn't come to Moses and say he was worried that Moses had bitten off more than he could chew, and that it might not end well. Rather, he spoke in certainties: this state of affairs would surely wear Moses and the people out. It's not any good for anyone when people think that they can handle all of the affairs of God by themselves. It simply cannot be done.

Jethro then gave Moses a solution:

Now obey my voice; I will give you advice, and God be with you! You shall represent the people before God and bring their cases to God, and you shall warn them about the statutes and the laws, and make them know the way in which they must walk and what they must do. Moreover, look for able men from all the people, men who fear God, who are trustworthy and hate a bribe, and place such men over the people as chiefs of thousands, of hundreds, of fifties, and of tens. And let them judge the people at all times. Every great matter they shall bring to you, but any small matter they shall decide themselves. So it will be easier for you, and they will bear the burden with you. If you do this, God will direct you, you will be able to endure, and all this people also will go to their place in peace. (vv. 19–23)

God moved Moses through Jethro to implement a careful organizational structure, not unlike a military organization, that would provide clear responsibility and a high degree of agility in reacting to circumstances. Jethro urged Moses to look for men who feared God and loved righteousness and to set them over the people as judges. The judges would hear the small cases and bring to Moses anything they couldn't handle. In this way, the burden would be spread among many.

We sometimes dismiss organization as something that secular people do. We want to have the spontaneous freedom of the Spirit. There's sometimes a subtle mistrust of careful planning, strategy, and organization in the church—but God Himself ordains that this kind of organization take place. Everyone is ministered to in it, everyone is accounted for, and all of the bases are covered.

In the book of Numbers, Moses finally implements this organizational process. In chapter 11, the people complain that they have no meat to eat. In the wilderness, there was no food. There was only scrub grass for their herds to graze on. There were no crops and no livestock for them to eat. They were subsisting daily on this miraculous provision from heaven, called manna, that God had given to them.

Manna for breakfast, manna for lunch, manna for dinner. If you want to have a midnight snack, manna.

So, the people began to pine for their slave-labor days in Egypt. They didn't remember the scourgings they received from their overseers or how nice it was when Pharaoh forced them to make bricks without straw. All they remembered were the good old days of the leeks, garlic, cucumbers, and onions—and they were ready to trade in their salvation for a cucumber.

Moses was at the end of his rope, and he appealed to the Lord, saying that leading this murmuring people was too great a burden for him to bear. In his distress, Moses prays, "If you will treat me like this, kill me at once, if I find favor in your sight, that I may not see my wretchedness" (Num. 11:15).

The Lord promised to give the people meat—but so much meat that they would be sick from it:

> You shall not eat just one day, or two days, or five days, or ten days, or twenty days, but a whole month, until it comes out at your nostrils and becomes loathsome to you, because you have rejected the LORD who is among you. (vv. 19–20)

The Lord also told Moses to gather seventy elders to bear the burden of leading the people. Then, we read:

> The LORD came down in the cloud and spoke to him, and took some of the Spirit that was on him and put it on the seventy elders. And as soon as the Spirit rested on them, they prophesied. But they did not continue doing it. Now two men remained in the camp, one named Eldad, and the other named Medad, and the Spirit rested on them. (v. 25)

Seeing these men prophesying, Joshua chimed in and said to Moses, "My lord Moses, stop them" (v. 28). The people were used to having only Moses being anointed by the Holy God. This looked like an insurrection to them: someone else was manifesting the power of God besides Moses.

It's crucial what Moses says to Joshua here. He says, "Are you jealous for my sake? Would that all the LORD's people were prophets, that the LORD would put his Spirit on them!" (v. 29). Moses saw that instead of one leader to bring the Israelites into the Promised Land, there were seventy-one. His prayer was that, someday, all of the Lord's people would be prophets, that at some point God would pour out His Spirit upon all men.

By the time we get to the prophet Joel, that prayer of Moses had become a prophecy. Joel said that the Lord declared, "And it shall come to pass afterward, that I will pour out my Spirit on all flesh; your sons and your daughters shall prophesy, your old men shall dream dreams, and your young men shall see visions" (Joel 2:28). At Pentecost, the prophecy of Joel was fulfilled and the Spirit was poured out upon the whole church (see Acts 2:14–21). No longer is the Spirit limited to a select few; He belongs to and indwells all believers.

The New Testament portrait of the church is that of an organization energized by God the Holy Spirit. In the New Testament doctrine of the church, every single person in the body of Christ has been enabled and energized by God the Holy Spirit to be battle ready—to be a part of the mission that God has given to His church. To look at the church as an organization where the labor and ministry are done only by the ministers is to miss the entire point. The ministers' primary task is to equip the saints—the rank-and-file, the people in the pews. The ministry of the church belongs to the people of God who have been gifted by the Holy Spirit to carry it out.

Chapter Four

Systematic Evangelism

Many Christians go their entire lives without being used by God to be the human instrument and means by which a person comes to Christ. My own calling is not as an evangelist, but seeing another human being come to Christ is the most meaningful ministry experience I've ever had.

I once was hired by a church to be the minister of theology, which meant that my job was to teach. They also added to my job description "minister of evangelism." I said I didn't know anything about evangelism. So, they sent me to a seminar to train in evangelism.

The minister leading the seminar talked about how to memorize an outline, how he uses key questions to stimulate discussion, and how there's a pattern to the way in which evangelism is to flow. The idea behind the method he used was to focus attention on the ultimate issue of a person's individual redemption—how can he justify himself before God? Most people will say that they have lived a good life; very few will say that they have been justified by faith alone in Christ alone.

Methods such as these have much to recommend them. They are easy to learn, and they make it possible for people to engage in discussions about Christianity, though care must be taken that one is not simply reading a script but rather is really connecting with the other person.

Ultimately, evangelism is less about the method one uses and more about the message one proclaims. Evangelism, remember, is the proclamation of the gospel—telling the story, announcing the news. Some fear that they don't know enough to evangelize. I say, "Tell them what you *do* know." Leave the defense of the truth claims to the apologist and hold forth the simple message of the gospel.

Anyone who has the ability to speak about three or four simple principles can become an effective evangelist. This is where evangelism programs and training can help.

The book of Acts tells us of Stephen, the first Christian martyr. He is stoned to death in chapter 7, upon which a terrible persecution breaks out. It looks as if the end of the nascent church might be near. But then we read:

> And Saul approved of his [Stephen's] execution. And there arose on that day a great persecution against the church in Jerusalem, and they were all scattered throughout the regions of Judea and Samaria, except the apostles. Devout men buried Stephen and made great lamentation over him. But Saul was ravaging the church, and entering house after house, he dragged off men and women and committed them to prison. Now those who were scattered went about preaching the word. (Acts 8:1–4)

How did the Christian church move from twelve people to an army? Then to a nation? Then to an entire empire, and eventually to become the greatest cultural influence in Western civilization? The secret is right there in the last verse:

"Those who were scattered went about preaching the word."

Who were they who were scattered abroad? There was a great persecution against the church at Jerusalem, and they were all scattered abroad, throughout the regions of Judea and Samaria—all except the Apostles. It was the rank-and-file believers who caused this enormous expansion of the early church.

Is there any structure to this spreading evangelism that we can find in the book of Acts? Yes—we see in the first chapter of Acts that the commission is given to the early church by Jesus: "You will receive power when the Holy Spirit has come upon you, and you will be my witnesses in Jerusalem and in all Judea and Samaria, and to the end of the earth" (Acts 1:8). This description follows the pattern of the Great Commission.

The Apostles and the early believers were also commissioned to make a specific announcement. When we analyze the preaching found in the book of Acts, we repeatedly see what theologians call the *kerygma,* or "proclamation," which is the same essential message in every sermon. This message consists of the basic realities of the death, resurrection, and ascension of Christ. Then, in addition to the *kerygma,* we find in the New Testament the emergence of what was called the *didachē*, or "teaching," which supplemented the initial proclamation of Christ's salvific work.

The organization of the church usually worked in this fashion: Christians went out and proclaimed the gospel. Other people responded to the gospel, were baptized, and then were immediately taught the content of the *didachē*. This was similar to what we might think of as learning a catechism or the essential teachings of the church. That's when new believers learned about the broad outlines of God's work in the world, from creation to the lives of Abraham, Isaac, and Jacob to His current work through Jesus Christ and the Holy Spirit. The church did not try to wait until the world was educated in Judaism or even in all of the theology of Christianity before calling the world to commitment to Christ.

Teaching is vitally important. But, generally speaking, it is best received *after* a person has responded to the gospel. We cannot educate people into the kingdom of God. Education is something that takes place after conversion. So, the New Testament church was mobilized, it was energized, and it had vision to go out and, in a very simple way, present the gospel and then follow up with teaching. I call this approach "systematic evangelism."

At my previous church, we began to visit people in their homes for the purpose of evangelism. When we identified ourselves as representatives of the Presbyterian church, the initial responses and assumptions of our hosts were that we were coming for money or inviting them for church membership. That's the only reason Presbyterians had ever visited them before. We would say, "We're not here to ask you for a pledge card. We're not here even to ask you to join our church. We're here to talk to you about Christ." It blew them away.

This approach was systematic, mobilized, and scheduled. At times, it seemed so mechanical and uninspiring. But we went, week after week, for a year and a half. We would come together as the church, then we would go out together in teams; before anybody set foot in that community, we had corporate prayer, kneeling and praying for every single person who went out into that community. They knew that the church was behind them in this mission. In the end, we met and explained the gospel to many people whom we might not have come across had we used a less systematic approach.

Chapter Five

The Biblical Basis for Missions

In the 1960s, some theologians believed that they saw in the New Testament a tension or conflict between God the Father and God the Son. In their view, God the Father is portrayed as an angry deity who only has room for wrath toward the world; He aimed to bring justice to bear by punishing the whole of mankind. On the other hand, God the Son, who is characterized by a much greater spirit of compassion and mercy and love, comes on the scene of history in order to persuade the Father to spare some of these wicked people and to induce the Father to redeem those for whom Christ laid down His life.

This view, however, is unsupported by the biblical evidence. Even a cursory reading of the Scriptures indicates that Jesus saw His mission and calling as that which *fulfills* the desire of the Father. His food and drink were to do the will of the Father; Jesus came into the world because He was sent into the world by the Father. It was the Father's idea to bring about redemption and to act on His concern and love for the world. So, He took action: He sent His only begotten Son. To think otherwise would be, at minimum, to undermine the very mission of the church itself.

The biblical basis for missions begins with God's work of sending His Son for our redemption. Nearly every local church has a portion of its budget designated for the task of missions. Most Christians have some idea of what mission means—but the *basis* for that mission may not be as clear.

What is mission, and what is the principal foundation for the mission of the church? The word *mission* itself comes from the Latin verb *missio*, which means "to send." So, literally, missions has to do with sending. In the Scriptures, we see the verb *to send* being used over and over, in a multitude of ways. But there's a sense in which the whole life of the church and the whole experience of the Christian are rooted ultimately in some kind of sending that is founded in the authority and the action of God Himself.

It is God who institutes, sanctifies, and mandates the mission of the church. One of the most famous passages in the Bible speaks to this mission: "For God so loved the world, that he gave his only Son, that whoever believes in him should not perish but have eternal life" (John 3:16). Many people know this verse, but how many know the next verse? "For God did not send his Son into the world to condemn the world, but in order that the world might be saved through him" (v. 17). The motive behind the divine action of redemption crystallized in John 3:16 lies in the action of God in sending His Son into the world. The purpose was not negative but positive; God didn't send the Son for the purpose of judgment, but rather for the purpose of redemption. Verse 34 reveals more about that mission: "For he whom God has sent utters the words of God, for he gives the Spirit without measure." Who is the one whom God had sent? It's Jesus Christ, and He was sent speaking the words of God and giving the Holy Spirit without measure.

Jesus speaks also in His High Priestly Prayer of speaking the words of God and of having been sent by the Father:

"For I have given them the words that you gave me, and they have received them and have come to know in truth that I came from you; and they have believed that you sent me" (John 17:8). As He continues to pray for the disciples, He says, "As you sent me into the world, so I have sent them into the world" (v. 18). Here we see the basis for the mission of the church. God sent Christ; Christ sent the church. The biblical basis for missions is the Word of God spoken in divine authority; it is the mandate of Christ.

We live in a time wherein the secular culture and many ecclesiastical authorities dismiss the whole concept of world missions. Some claim that the time of world missionary activity is over. One argument offered for this is that missions are not only unnecessary but are a destructive force unleashed upon the world. The charge is that world missions have been nothing more than a platform for imperialism and for the exploitation of the underdeveloped nations by the industrialized nations in the world. There is also the sociological consideration that civilization is a corrupting influence upon innocent natives who would have greater well-being and peace without the problems of the Western world that are inevitably carried in the carpetbags of the missionary.

This is pure nonsense, of course, and not supported by evidence. Modern missions provide valuable medical, educational, and agricultural resources, in addition to the important work of preaching the gospel. Unfortunately, the number of missionaries in the field continues to decline, because a significant portion of the church no longer believes that it's necessary to fulfill the mandate from Christ to carry the gospel to the ends of the earth.

But the mission of God has always been a sending program. God spoke to Abram in the land of the Chaldeans and sent him to a new land where he would be the father of a great nation. He came to Moses in the midst of the Midianite wilderness and sent Moses to Pharaoh with the message, "Let my people go." God sent His children out of Egypt and into the Promised Land. When they were disobedient to the covenant that God had made with them, He sent the prophets to warn them. When that didn't bring them around, He sent His Son.

The word *apostle* means "one who is sent." In the time of the New Testament, an apostle was one who would carry the authority to speak in the name of the one who had sent him. In the New Testament, the first Apostle is Christ Himself, the one sent by the Father. Then, the Father and

Son sent the Holy Spirit. Then, the Spirit was poured out on the church, and the church was sent to complete the ministry of Christ in all the world—to every tongue, to every nation, to every tribe.

In Romans 10, Paul raises a series of questions that speak directly to the matter of our responsibility. Having affirmed that "everyone who calls on the name of the Lord will be saved" (v. 13), he then asks:

> How then will they call on him in whom they have not believed? And how are they to believe in him of whom they have never heard? And how are they to hear without someone preaching? And how are they to preach unless they are sent? As it is written, "How beautiful are the feet of those who preach the good news!" (vv. 14–15)

No one can call upon Christ to save them if they don't believe in Him. Paul puts his finger on the challenge and the responsibility of the church: to send, so that people might hear about Christ, and upon hearing, might believe and be saved.

When is the missionary mandate over? When it has

been fulfilled, and the mandate of Christ has been completed. If someone stands up in a church meeting and says that the day of mission is over, resist him with all of your might, because that person is advocating nothing less than treason to the Lord of the church. It is the church's duty to fulfill the Great Commission, to send people into all the world. That's what missions is all about.

Chapter Six

Seeking
the Lost

One day when we were living in Pennsylvania, our dog ran away from home. I loved my dog, so I didn't just sit at home and whistle. I set out on foot, and then in the car, to search for my lost dog. I had to go around the outskirts of the Ligonier Valley Study Center, situated in the mountains in a rather remote area. It's not like the suburbs where you look out your window and see into the window of your next-door neighbor. Many homes were situated on ten-, fifty-, or even hundred-acre lots. The houses were widely separated from each other; we didn't know everyone who lived up and down the street.

In that area, there were two types of people. One type was those who were very rich, who used the area as a summer resort. Another type was people who were desperately poor: the "Appalachian mountain people." They lived virtually side by side with the extravagantly wealthy. As I was looking for my dog, I began to go down roads and driveways that I'd never traveled before. The one impression that I carry with me from that experience was coming out the end of my driveway, turning right onto the street, and going less than a quarter of a mile before turning down a driveway that I had passed probably a thousand times.

I had no idea what was at the end of that driveway, but I couldn't believe what was there. It was as if I had stepped into a different century or another world—a world of abject poverty. I saw people living without food, without adequate shelter, and without sufficient clothing; they were obviously unemployed and barely eking out an existence. I had no idea those people even lived there, and yet, their residence was less than two thousand feet from my house.

I'd been there eight or nine years without realizing that they lived right across the street from me.

It's easy for us to shield ourselves—not consciously, not maliciously—but nevertheless, to pass on the other side in order to remain unaware of the pain and the spiritual hopelessness that is around us. That was not the way of Jesus. He looked for the pain. He searched for lost people. That was the first step in redeeming them.

Jesus gained a reputation for associating with those who were considered outcasts. Pariahs, undesirables, the unlovely of the Jewish culture—all these gathered around Jesus. This disturbed the Pharisees and scribes, the dignitaries and clergy of the day. They had adopted a tradition that taught salvation by segregation: keep yourself away from anyone who is involved in sin; that is how you can secure your own redemption. It was part of their working philosophy to isolate themselves from those who were sinners. Jesus came and defied that tradition by openly associating with the pariahs of the culture.

It was on one of these occasions that the Pharisees began to grumble and complain about Jesus' companions. In response, Jesus tells a series of parables, the first of which reads as follows:

What man of you, having a hundred sheep, if he has lost one of them, does not leave the ninety-nine in the open country, and go after the one that is lost, until he finds it? And when he has found it, he lays it on his shoulders, rejoicing. And when he comes home, he calls together his friends and his neighbors, saying to them, "Rejoice with me, for I have found my sheep that was lost." Just so, I tell you, there will be more joy in heaven over one sinner who repents than over ninety-nine righteous persons who need no repentance. (Luke 15:4–7)

This parable is called "the parable of the lost sheep." There are those today who don't believe that anyone is lost; they reject the whole concept of being lost. There are those who are universalists, who believe everyone goes to heaven automatically; justification is not by faith or works, but simply by death—because no one is truly lost. Then there are those who say that, given enough time, lost people will eventually find their way back. We just need to leave them alone.

However, if no one is lost, or if they will find their way back on their own, then the mission of Christ was a waste of time; the atonement of Christ was not needed. This casts a shadow upon the whole mission of Jesus Himself.

Jesus defined His mission by saying, "The Son of Man came to seek and to save the lost" (Luke 19:10). He didn't simply say that He came to *save* the lost, but that He came to *seek* and to save them. That is, before the lost can be redeemed, they must first be found.

It is finding the lost that necessitates the endeavor of missions. It's easy for us to deceive ourselves into thinking that no one is lost, and one way of doing that is to distance ourselves from the search—that is, to make sure that we keep ourselves uninformed about the needs of the lost, to insulate ourselves from knowing what is really going on in the world. For instance, we don't go out of our way to understand and learn about all of the people who are starving in this world. When we are confronted with it, our consciences are pricked and we are moved to action. But we don't go out of our way to find misery; we think there's enough misery in our own lives, without looking for more.

When I was a child, it was still normal for the doctor to make house calls, where he would actually come to your house. Every day, he would drive through the community and visit children, the elderly, or whoever was sick. Today, if you're sick, the doctor is not going to come to you; you have go to the doctor. Unfortunately, many churches operate the same way; they hang out a shingle and invite people to come to them.

But Jesus didn't have a building; He didn't wait behind closed doors for people to come and see Him. His was a ministry of "walking around." He went out to where the people were. That's what missions is all about. The ministry of Christ was a ministry of searching for pain and for those who are lost.

The second parable that Jesus tells the Pharisees reads as follows:

Or what woman, having ten silver coins, if she loses one coin, does not light a lamp and sweep the house and seek diligently until she finds it? And when she has found it, she calls together her friends and neighbors, saying, "Rejoice with me, for I have found the coin that I had lost." Just so, I tell you, there is joy before the angels of God over one sinner who repents. (vv. 8–10)

Maybe this is the only time the woman has ever swept the house. She's lost something, and she will turn over everything to find a tenth of her fortune. She lost one coin, and she didn't just miss it and say, "That's all right; I have nine coins left." She moved heaven and earth to find that coin.

Did you ever lose something valuable that was important to you? If so, then you know that inner panic you feel as you try to find it. I remember when I was living in the home of a friend who was back in the Netherlands finishing his doctoral dissertation. Before he left for the Netherlands, he gave me a key to his safe deposit box. He said, "If I ever have an emergency, I will contact you. I have funds set aside in this safe deposit box. If something comes up, all you have to do is take that key to the bank, get out the box, and wire me the money."

Several months passed, and I got an urgent message saying that he needed money desperately. I went right into my desk where I knew I had put the key, opened up the drawer in the center section, looked down—and the key was gone. I had no idea where it was. I searched the house frantically. I couldn't find it. I went to the bank and explained the situation. They said, "We're sorry. Without that key, we are not allowed to let you in here to open that box."

I explained the situation to my students in my class. I had my whole class come to my house, and we went over that house with a fine-toothed comb. We lifted up the rugs. We went through the winter clothes. We took out the drawers. We ruffled the curtains. We systematically went through every square inch of that house.

Eventually, after much searching, I found that key. When I found it, I went nuts. I was leaping for joy, jumping up and down—and I thought, here I am rejoicing over finding a key. I rejoiced also when I found my lost dog. What does heaven do when a lost person is found? There is more joy in heaven over one sinner who repents that over ninety-nine righteous people who need no repentance.

I get excited when I find my lost dog. I get excited when I find a key that is lost. I get excited when I find some money that is lost. Heaven has a feast when a lost person is found. We will look for keys. We will look for coins. We will look for sheep. Why won't we look for people?

If you've ever been lost in the woods, you know what a terrible feeling it is. It's easy to make one turn, then another; then, suddenly, the landmarks all look the same and you become disoriented. You can start moving farther away from the point of recognition, getting deeper into the woods without knowing it. The realization that you are lost can be terrifying. But even more terrifying, there are those who are lost who don't even know it.

One of my favorite illustrations of this idea comes from *Alice in Wonderland*. Alice is walking along and doesn't know where she's going. She comes to a fork in the road and doesn't know which way to go. She's paralyzed with indecision, and sitting up in the tree is the Cheshire Cat, grinning from ear to ear. Alice finds a bit of encouragement by the presence of the Cheshire Cat, and she asks him, "Which way should I go?"

The cat says, "Well, it depends. Where are you heading?"

Alice says, "I don't know."

The cat says, "Then it doesn't matter which way you go."

Many people today are like that. They have no idea where they are and no clue where they're going. Their whole lives consist of wandering about aimlessly, without purpose, design, meaning, or significance. It's one thing to be lost; it's another to be lost and not know it. When a person is in that state, it is inevitable that they will experience a crisis and realize they have no idea where they are or how they got there.

God puts a priority on seeking people like that. After the lost coin and the lost sheep, Jesus turns His attention to people. The parable of the prodigal son (Luke 15:11–32) is a familiar story, and it's important to keep the focus where it belongs: not on the lost son, but on the father and his great joy at the repentance and return of the son. When the father sees his son far off, he races down the road and embraces him, kills the fatted calf, gives the signet ring to him, and clothes him with a cloak of honor. As he says to the older brother, "It was fitting to celebrate and be glad, for this your brother was dead, and is alive; he was lost, and is found" (v. 32).

This parable tells us what God is like. He runs after the lost, and He rejoices when one person is redeemed.

That is the mission of the church, and each of us has a responsibility to make sure that the lost are sought and found. We're not dealing with coins or sheep, and we're not dealing with dogs or keys. We are dealing with people whom Christ loves. He said so Himself.

About the Author

Dr. R.C. Sproul was founder of Ligonier Ministries, founding pastor of Saint Andrew's Chapel in Sanford, Fla., first president of Reformation Bible College, and executive editor of *Tabletalk* magazine. His radio program, *Renewing Your Mind,* is still broadcast daily on hundreds of radio stations around the world and can also be heard online. He was author of more than one hundred books, including *The Holiness of God, Chosen by God,* and *Everyone's a Theologian.* He was recognized throughout the world for his articulate defense of the inerrancy of Scripture and the need for God's people to stand with conviction upon His Word.

Free eBooks *by* R.C. Sproul

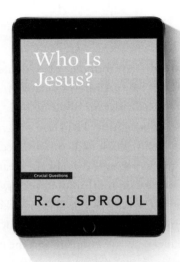

Does prayer really change things? Can I be sure I'm saved? Dr. R.C. Sproul answers these important questions, along with more than thirty others, in his Crucial Questions series. Designed for the Christian or thoughtful inquirer, these booklets can be used for personal study, small groups, and conversations with family and friends. Browse the collection and download your free digital ebooks today.

Get 3 free months of *Tabletalk*

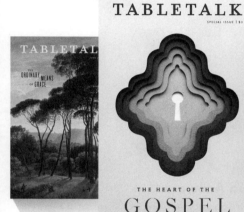

In 1977, R.C. Sproul started *Tabletalk* magazine.
Today it has become the most widely read subscriber-based monthly
devotional magazine in the world. **Try it free for 3 months.**

𝕋 TryTabletalk.com/CQ | 800-435-4343

ASK LIGONIER

Do we have free will?

Does prayer change things?

Is it true that God controls everything?

A Place to Find Answers

Maybe you're leading a Bible study tomorrow. Maybe you're just beginning to dig deeper. It's good to know that you can always ask Ligonier. For more than fifty years, Christians have been looking to Ligonier Ministries, the teaching fellowship of R.C. Sproul, for clear and helpful answers to biblical and theological questions. Now you can ask those questions online as they arise, confident that our team will work quickly to provide clear, concise, and trustworthy answers. The *Ask Ligonier* podcast provides another avenue for you to submit questions to some of the most trusted pastors and teachers who are serving the church today. When you have questions, just ask Ligonier.